Lafayette

HERO OF TWO NATIONS

by Keith Brandt
illustrated by Scott Snow

Troll Associates

Library of Congress Cataloging-in-Publication Data

Brandt, Keith, (date)
  Lafayette, hero of two nations / by Keith Brandt; illustrated by
Scott Snow.
     p.   cm.
  Summary: A brief biography of one of early America's greatest
friends and defenders, Gilbert du Motier.
    ISBN 0-8167-1771-0 (lib. bdg.)   ISBN 0-8167-1772-9 (pbk.)
    1. Lafayette, Marie Joseph Paul Yves Roch Gilbert du Motier,
marquis de, 1757-1834—Juvenile literature. 2. France—
History—1789-1815—Juvenile literature. 3. Generals—France—
Biography—Juvenile literature. 4. France. Armée—Biography—
Juvenile literature. 5. Generals—United States—Biography—
Juvenile literature. 6. United States. Army—Biography—Juvenile
literature. 7. Statesmen—France—Biography—Juvenile literature.
8. United States—History—Revolution, 1775-1783—Participation,
French—Juvenile literature. [1. Lafayette, Marie Joseph Paul Yves
Roch Gilbert du Motier, marquis de, 1757-1834. 2. Generals.
3. Statesmen. 4. United States—History—Revolution, 1775-1783—
Biography.] I. Snow, Scott, ill. II. Title.
DC146.L2B73   1990
944.04'092—dc20
[B]
[92]   89-33981

Lafayette

HERO OF TWO NATIONS

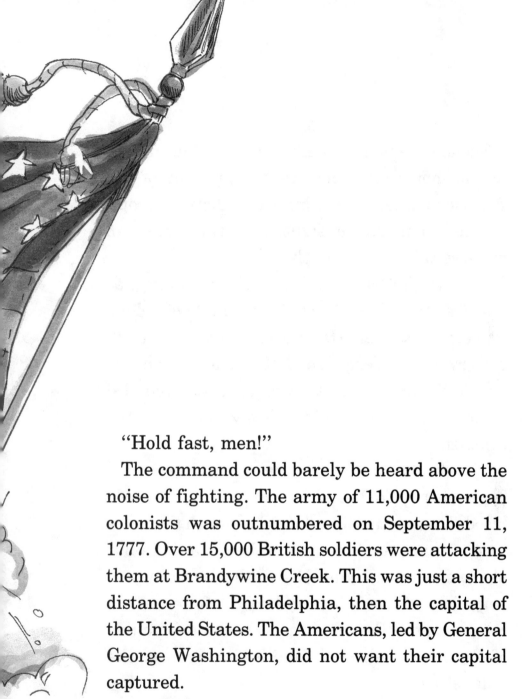

"Hold fast, men!"

The command could barely be heard above the noise of fighting. The army of 11,000 American colonists was outnumbered on September 11, 1777. Over 15,000 British soldiers were attacking them at Brandywine Creek. This was just a short distance from Philadelphia, then the capital of the United States. The Americans, led by General George Washington, did not want their capital captured.

5

Suddenly, a young man of twenty galloped forth on his horse. He rode up to the front of the American line, challenging the British troops. It was an inspiring sight. And the American soldiers rallied to hold the line.

Who was he? He wasn't American. But he was one of America's greatest friends and defenders, Gilbert du Motier. He is better known through history as the Marquis de Lafayette. And on this day, in the Battle of Brandywine, he was wounded in the leg as he fought side by side with the colonists.

Gilbert du Motier was born in France on September 6, 1757. Both his parents were of noble blood. That's why Gilbert was born with the noble title of marquis. It is ranked below a duke but above an earl or count. His mother's family was very rich. Gilbert's father, Michel Motier, was a colonel in the French Army. He came from one of the most respected families in France, the Lafayettes.

When Gilbert was almost two years old, his father was killed in battle. It was during a war between France and Great Britain. The war had started a few months before Gilbert was born. Colonel Lafayette was called to serve soon after the war began. He was not home when his son was born, but he did see the baby during a few visits.

Sadly, Gilbert never really knew his father. All he knew were the stories of the brave soldier who died fighting the British. His father's courage and devotion to duty inspired Gilbert for the rest of his life.

From the time he was born, Gilbert lived at the chateau of Chavaniac. This large house belonged to his father's parents. Young Gilbert was raised there by his grandparents. After his father died, his mother moved to Paris, where she lived with her family. This was normal for French nobility. Even if Gilbert's father had lived, the boy would not have spent much time with his parents.

Still, Gilbert's early childhood was not like the early childhoods of most nobles. He stayed in the rich comfort of Chavaniac with his grandparents. But in other noble families, a baby was usually sent to live with a peasant family. The child stayed with that family until the age of four or five. Then the child was brought back to his or her own home. But even then, the child was raised by servants. Children of the nobility were not to be seen or heard.

Adults of the nobility spent all their time at the court of the king and queen. They had to if they hoped to receive special favors and a salary from the royal treasury. Nobles in France were paid great sums of money for being a lady in waiting, a captain of the guard, a superintendent of the queen's household, a governor or governess to the royal children, and so on. There were dozens of court jobs for the nobility. These jobs took no work. They were just titles, yet they were worth a lot of money.

Court positions were passed from father to son and from mother to daughter. Noble families felt that they owned these positions. They did not want to give up the money and favors that went with them.

That is why Gilbert's mother stayed at the court of King Louis the Fifteenth. It was her way of keeping the family position in the family. If she stayed at Chavaniac, someone else would take her position and the money that came with it. So, Madame de Lafayette was not a bad mother for leaving her son with his father's parents. She was a good mother because she was protecting her child's future.

Little Gilbert was cared for by a grandmother who adored him. Grandmother du Motier gave him a lot of love. She also gave him a wonderful feeling about his father. Through her words, Gilbert was able to imagine his father fearless in the face of the enemy. Day by day, the little boy was taught to see his father as a great man.

Gilbert knew he must grow up to do great deeds. Papa had been a hero. The history of the Lafayette family was filled with great soldiers, judges, scholars, and leaders of the church. The name of Lafayette was honored throughout France. Gilbert saw proof of this every day. All the people on the family estate showed Gilbert deep respect. All the peasants, young and old, bowed to him and took off their hats when he passed by.

There was one time, however, when Gilbert thought he wasn't being shown the proper respect.

He screamed at a stable hand who did not bring Gilbert's horse fast enough. "I will send him away!" Gilbert told his grandmother. "I am the marquis! He must obey me!"

"No, Gilbert," Madame du Motier said. "You will not send him away. A true nobleman does not dismiss a servant for such a small thing. His family has served our family loyally for four generations. You must return their loyalty by being a fair master. They take their hats off not to please a silly little boy, but to show respect for the name of Lafayette. And you must earn that respect."

Gilbert's education began when he was five years old. His first teacher was a Jesuit priest, who taught him to read and write. Most of all, he tried to teach the little boy right from wrong. In the two years the priest was with him, Gilbert learned some important lessons. He learned to think before acting. He also learned to respect honesty. And he learned that goodness and fairness mean more than wealth and titles.

When Gilbert was seven, he got a new teacher, Abbé Fayon. This priest was a very strict teacher. He made sure that Gilbert did his lessons thoroughly. Abbé Fayon set high standards. He did not think that reading and writing with correct grammar and spelling were enough. He felt that Gilbert must learn to write with good sense in fine language. To do this, the boy had to think clearly and logically. Sometimes this meant writing an essay again and again until it was good enough for the teacher.

The way Abbé Fayon taught Gilbert was unusual. That's because education in eighteenth-century France was not like it is today. Only men and women of the church had to be educated. Poor people received no schooling at all.

Royalty and nobility were *not* expected to know the school subjects Gilbert learned. If a child of a noble family knew some arithmetic or quoted a line of poetry, it was considered charming. But it wasn't considered necessary. It was more important to ride well, dance well, and talk well.

A boy of a noble family spent a great deal of time learning to shoot and to fence. Nobles did not work. Their lives were spent at different kinds of play. So their childhoods were devoted to learning to play with grace and style.

Young Gilbert spent his afternoons riding, shooting, fencing, and doing everything else expected of a young gentleman. But his mornings were filled with lessons. In addition to reading, writing, and arithmetic, Gilbert learned English.

Abbé Fayon hated all things English. But he believed it was important to know about France's enemy. That included learning the enemy's language. Gilbert shared this hatred of England because his father had been killed by an English cannonball. It was why Gilbert did not want to learn English. But the abbé insisted that he do so.

Years later, Lafayette was grateful to his teacher. As an aide to General George Washington, the young man needed to know English. It was also important to his becoming the main contact between the Continental Congress and the king of France.

Abbé Fayon's teachings shaped Gilbert in other ways. But some of these ways were not intended by the teacher. Fayon believed that slavery was right, that the king had absolute power over the people, and that there should be no freedom of speech, religion, or the press. Fayon wanted his student to believe what he believed. But here the abbé failed. Even as a boy, Gilbert was developing a strong sense of justice and equality.

When he was eleven, Gilbert was sent to Paris. There, he lived with his mother and her family at court. This move to the French capital changed Gilbert's life. He was a country boy used to a quiet, easy life. Paris was a noisy, busy, crowded place. It was the center of trade and ideas for all of Europe. Paris set the style and everyone else followed. It was true of clothing, music, books, dances, food, sports, and furniture. These were all part of Gilbert's new life. Suddenly, he'd have to learn how to behave with witty, worldly people.

Gilbert was stunned to meet his mother. He had not seen her for eight years. She was a dazzling figure in her silk and lace dress. Her high, powdered wig was adorned with ostrich feathers and glittery jewels. Madame de Lafayette walked as if she were gliding from cloud to cloud. And her voice was so soft and sweet that Gilbert felt he should whisper in her presence.

Gilbert also met his grandfather, the Marquis de la Rivière, and other members of his mother's family. The boy was overwhelmed by their fine manners and splendid clothing. It made him feel foolish and out of place. But very soon, Gilbert wore proper court clothing too.

Proper court clothing for a boy meant a brightly colored coat of silk or velvet with gold buttons and fancy lining. The trousers Gilbert wore to just below his knees were a different-colored silk. His vest had designs in still another color. Under the vest, he wore a white shirt with lace at the collar and sleeves. His stockings were also white. And like all young gentlemen of that time, Gilbert

wore a powdered wig. At court, young Gilbert was as flashy a dresser as any nobleman. But later as a man, after he had been to America, he dressed more simply. He was never really happy in silk and lace.

Gilbert's grandfather soon had him named to a regiment of the king's musketeers. These were the French royal household bodyguards. At the same time, the eleven-year-old was enrolled at the Collège du Plessis. He attended this school for four years. Gilbert studied Latin, Greek, mathematics, history, geography, and literature. He did well in English and Latin, but best in fencing and horsemanship. He was an average student in the other subjects.

Gilbert was not happy at the school. In many ways, he was still a country boy, while most of his classmates had spent their whole lives in the city. They knew the right things to say and do, and what not to say and do. Gilbert felt awkward and shy around them. It took him a long time to make friends. Most of his four years at Plessis were spent alone. He longed for each summer vacation when he could go back to Chavaniac.

In March 1770, when Gilbert was twelve, his mother died. A few months later, his grandfather, the Marquis de la Rivière, died. The wealth

Gilbert received after their deaths made him one of the richest people in France. It was a turning point in his life.

Gilbert was in the legal care of his great-grandfather. But he was really on his own. Other nobles with so much money and freedom often became useless and wasteful playboys. Gilbert, however, became more responsible and thoughtful.

The young man stayed in school until the summer of 1772. Now his vacations were spent serving as a lieutenant in the musketeers, and as a member of the Royal Guard. Only noblemen of the highest rank were Royal Guardsmen. They rode with the king on hunts. Members of the Royal Guard were close to the king and trusted by him. For this reason, they had great influence over French policy.

Gilbert's teen-age years were very busy. He spent part of each year with his military regiment. During another part of the year, he attended a riding academy. Still another portion of the year was spent on the estate at Chavaniac. He also found time to practice swordsmanship with a fencing master and to attend parties and dances at court.

Gilbert was still in his teens when he fell in love with Adrienne de Noailles. She was the daughter of the Duc d'Ayen, whose family was as rich as Gilbert's family. It was considered a perfect match. It was also an unusual match.

The marriage was arranged by their families. This was the normal way for children of the nobility to marry. It had nothing to do with love. But Gilbert and Adrienne were very much in love. That is what made their marriage so unusual for the time. Gilbert was sixteen and Adrienne was fourteen when they were wed. It was a love that lasted for the rest of their lives.

In 1775, word reached France about the American Revolution. Most French nobles paid no attention to this news. But a small group was excited. This group of young nobles included Gilbert, Adrienne's brother, and several others. These young men met regularly at the Lafayette apartment in Paris. They talked about the causes of the war. They discussed the fight for freedom, as well as the hatred for Great Britain they shared with the American colonists.

During the next year, a fierce desire grew in Lafayette. The American Revolution was a cause worth fighting for. It was a way to use his wealth for the good of humanity. Above all, it was a way to become a great battlefield hero, like his father.

Gilbert convinced several close friends to join him. Then, in 1776, he took his plan to Silas Deane. Mr. Deane was the American representative to the court of France. Lafayette told Deane that he and his friends wanted to fight on the side of the colonists. Lafayette promised to pay for all uniforms and equipment. He would also pay for the ship that would carry the French volunteers across the Atlantic Ocean. All Lafayette wanted in return was to be made an officer in the Continental Army.

Silas Deane was delighted! It was December 1776, and the war was going hard for the colonists. Congress was running out of money. George Washington's army was pinned down near the Delaware River in Pennsylvania. His troops were cold and hungry, and many of them were eager to return home.

Lafayette's group was well fed, well armed, brave, and ready for battle. The news that they were coming lifted the spirits of the colonists. But there was something even more important about Lafayette's offer to fight. It was a signal that France supported the new United States of America. Great Britain would now know that the new nation did not stand alone in its fight for freedom.

King Louis the Sixteenth of France, however, was not a great lover of liberty. He had been a tyrant ever since he became king in 1774. But he did hate the British. And Lafayette was a former Royal Guardsman, a friend. For these reasons, the king was happy to do a favor for Lafayette.

The Continental Congress was quick to respond to Gilbert's offer. He was made a major general in the Continental Army. Gilbert gathered his fifteen volunteers and told them to make ready. Then he bought a ship, called the *Victoire*, a French word for "victory." Lafayette hired a captain and a crew. He bought provisions for the voyage and more than enough supplies for his volunteers. The *Victoire* set sail for America in April 1777. Two months later, it landed at Charleston, South Carolina.

Major General Lafayette was taken on a tour of the local fort. He was impressed by the fort itself. But he was horrified by the condition of the American troops. They were wearing ragged uniforms. Most of them had no boots. Their weapons were in poor condition, and their supply of ammunition was low. Right then, Lafayette gave the fort commander enough money to clothe and arm a hundred men.

After a few days in Charleston, Lafayette and his fifteen companions started north. They were on their way to Philadelphia to meet with the Continental Congress. It was an exciting journey for the French volunteers. The wilderness they traveled through was full of bears, deer, and other wildlife. And they met Indians along the way.

Still, the month-long trip was hard. Back home in their own country, the French noblemen were used to being waited on by servants. They lived in luxury there. But here in America, they slept out in the open. They cooked their own meals over campfires. They hunted not for sport but for that day's food. They slogged through miles of mud and thick growth. And yet they loved every minute of it. As Lafayette wrote home, "The United States is the most marvelous land on earth!"

It was the summer of 1777 when Lafayette reached Philadelphia. Right away, he arranged to meet with members of the Continental Congress. They were shocked to see how young he was. They expected an older, experienced officer and were cool toward him. But Lafayette had not come this far to be turned away. He wrote a letter to the Continental Congress. It said, "After the sacrifices that I have made in this cause, I have the right to ask two favors at your hands: the one is, to serve without pay, at my own expense; and the other, that I be allowed to serve at first as a volunteer in the ranks."

The Continental Congress was very impressed. The young nobleman was willing to be an ordinary foot soldier. He did not make demands because of his wealth and importance. He was ready to risk his life for America. So, a meeting was arranged between Lafayette and General George Washington. The two men got along

immediately. That meeting marked the beginning
of a lifelong friendship. Washington spoke of
Lafayette as "the boy" and treated him like a son.
Gilbert always called the general "my father."

The Battle of Brandywine in September 1777 was Lafayette's first taste of war. A short time later, he was with General Washington at Valley Forge, Pennsylvania. This was where the American Army stayed during the bitter winter of 1777-1778. Many of the soldiers suffered from frostbite and disease there. Lafayette remained with them throughout that winter, doing what he could to keep their hopes up. And in June 1778, the young Frenchman showed great bravery in leading a division of American troops against the British at Monmouth, New Jersey.

The young marquis was now a hero in two countries, the United States and France. And for the rest of the war, he continued to live up to that heroic beginning. Part of the time, Lafayette was in France, collecting money, men, supplies, and ships for Washington. But most of the time, he was in the United States, commanding troops in the field. The final days of the war in 1781 saw Lafayette heading the Continental Army of Virginia. He had indeed become the hero he had set out to be.

The American Revolution inspired the citizens of France to seek liberty in their own country. Lafayette shared their feelings. But he hoped for a peaceful revolution. Unfortunately, the French Revolution was a bloody and terrible time. Thousands of the nobility were executed. The royal family met the same fate. So did many of Lafayette's friends and relations, including his wife's entire family. Lafayette, still a national hero, was spared. So were his wife and children.

Lafayette spent his later years at his Chavaniac estate. Many times, he was invited to return to the United States and live out the rest of his life in honor there. He was even given special citizenship by the United States and by several individual states. Lafayette was pleased that he had been asked. But he turned down the invitations. He said the United States did not need him, but France did. Still, his heart remained in America, and he said he would be buried in American soil.

When Lafayette died on May 20, 1834, his wish was fulfilled. Though he was buried in Picpus Cemetery in Paris, the soil was American. Ten years before, following a visit to America, Lafayette had brought back a box holding the earth of his beloved adopted country. This soil became his final resting place.

The name of the Marquis de Lafayette lives on as a symbol of French-American friendship. Early in the twentieth century, the United States came to the aid of France against Germany. On July 4, 1917, during World War I, a ceremony was held to celebrate that friendship. It took place at Lafayette's tomb. That day, an American officer spoke the words "Lafayette, we are here!" It was America's way of saying thank you to the French hero of the American Revolution.

The legend of Lafayette does not end there. An American flag was placed at Lafayette's grave on the day he was buried in 1834. An American flag has flown there ever since. Even during World War II, it did not come down. When German troops marched into Paris in 1940, the flag continued to fly. And it was still there when the Allies liberated Paris from the Germans in 1944. To this day, an American flag flies over the tomb of Lafayette—as if his legend will live forever.

Index